Yosemite of My Heart

Poems of Adventures in California

Lalit Kumar

AOS Publishing, 2024

Copyright © 2024

Lalit Kumar

ISBN: 978-1-990496-53-0

Cover Design: Jessica James

Visit AOS Publishing's website:
www.aospublishing.com

Dedicated To

My Family, Friends and All Adventure Aficionados

"Walk away quietly in any direction and taste the freedom of the mountaineer. Camp out among the grasses and gentians of glacial meadows, in craggy garden nooks full of nature's darlings. Climb the mountains and get their good tidings, Nature's peace will flow into you as sunshine flows into trees. The winds will blow their own freshness into you and the storms their energy, while cares will drop off like autumn leaves. As age comes on, one source of enjoyment after another is closed, but nature's sources never fail."

~ John Muir

Table of Contents

Acknowledgement

I would like to sincerely thank my family and friends who supported me as this book took shape. Some of them would often be kind enough to be my primary critics and provide their honest feedback. I would also like to thank the 'Poetry of Diaspora' group in the San Francisco Bay Area, a community of like-minded people to share and exchange ideas with.

Foreword

In his book *Yosemite of My Heart, Poems of Adventures in California*, Lalit Kumar shares his passion for Nature and outdoors, always finding the poetic in the experience and in the language about it. That language carries readers along with him on his adventures to Yosemite, Big Sur, Mt. Whitney, and the Beat poets' San Francisco city and beyond. This is the perfect collection for both readers who are familiar with California and those who have never been there, at the same time skeptical of modern poetry but with an appetite for novelty and discovery of new territory—they will not put it down and come back to it as reference to historical and emotional connection again and again.

Terry Lucas,
Poet Laureate Emeritus of Marin County, California

Preface

It was the summer of 2007 when I came to California and was quickly smitten by its diversity in landscape, friendly people and cool Mediterranean-type climate. Since that day, I have lived in the San Francisco Bay Area and called California home. It gave me an opportunity to explore the state's various landmarks and indulge in my hobby for adventures and outdoors.

This book is borne out of the various experiences that I have had over the years, which has taken me Hiking in the Redwoods, Mountaineering in Mt Whitney & Mt. Shasta, Motorcycling through the cities of San Francisco & Sausalito, Kayaking in Channel Islands, Skiing in Tahoe, Horse Riding in Half Moon Bay, and various other adventures. Undoubtedly, California has an abundant playground with landscapes ranging from mountains, deserts, islands, meadows, lakes, rivers to ocean, providing a lavish palette of colors for every poet to experiment with the different strokes on his canvas. As an inveterate explorer and adventurer at heart, I have used 'Yosemite' in the title of this book as an anthropomorphic metaphor to convey the attributes of resiliency, persistence and staying strong despite the challenging circumstances, which are crucial to living a rich life.

Leafing through the book, you will find poems that delve into the distinctive 'California vibe' and unique essence of its varied and famous locations and landmarks. The Golden State's influence on USA and probably the whole world is quite impressive – consider the collective impact of technology break-through emanating from Silicon Valley, the creativity and story-telling dominance of Hollywood, its unmatched Natural beauty and a crucible of liberal and progressive ideas, all these make for quite a compelling story to be told. In addition, I am tempted to say that visiting a place leaves its imprint on our mind, not only in terms of its uniqueness, but also the thoughts & feelings that we are going through internally at that point of time, which could be directly or indirectly attributed to the influence of that location, in particular. You may find some resonance of this aspect of a place, in the poems as well.

It may seem that this poetry collection has placed more emphasis on San Francisco Bay area as its muse. That's not by design though; it so happens that I live in its vicinity. Moreover, I find the area to be rich in landmarks, literary history and pretty amenable to poetry. To me, San Francisco is a city built on an eternal quest, right from the days of 1849's gold rush to the San Francisco Renaissance in the late 1940s , leading up to 1950's Beat generation who came here looking for creativity and freedom of self-expression and found it in the air of 'the City'. Poetry and music were integral part of the bohemian culture that followed in its wake. The Haight-Ashbury's unique conglomeration of artists, poets, writers, musicians in 1960s gave the world, the Beat Poetry and the unique San Francisco sound (music) with Jefferson Airplane, Grateful Dead and possibly Metallica, as few examples. I welcome you, all the readers, to read through this poetry book with the above context and background in mind. And if these pages inspire you to embark on your own journey of exploring outdoors, nature and adventure, no matter where you live and how time starved you are, I would consider my muse's work accomplished.

Lalit Kumar
Santa Clara, January 2024

Yosemite of My Heart

Music resonates across the vale,
Concert stage set ablaze
In thunderous delight, Daybreak.
Yosemite Valley—
Meadows and the Merced—
Wakes up gradually, waits in a dream.

Half Dome,
Rocks like a lead guitarist,
Plucks strings, plays frets
Of the grand castle.
El Capitan
Provides the Bass,
Cathedral Rocks
Rounds out the rhythms
Of soulful Rock n Roll.
Bridal Veil Falls
Gushes forth a drum beat, crashing
Winds bring the cymbals.

This Tunnel View*
And Yosemite of my heart,
Intertwine in glorious sights and sounds
Streaming, surging, rising in crescendo.

Wild Yosemite,
Of solid granite walls,
Standing steady to the passing millennia —
Singe me with adventurous ardor!

O, for the distance I traveled,
Traversed miles and lengths and breadths
Yosemite in changing seasons
Yosemite in dawns and dusks.
Though I wonder of its splendor
Yet unseen, horizon unexplored
Its vistas tattooed on my naked eyes
Its sound abuzz in my listening ears.

Footnote: *Tunnel View is a panoramic vista in Yosemite National Park. The dramatic photography of Ansel Adams helped to make Tunnel View well renowned

Moving to California

That California, unknown to me—
Earthquake jolts and thousand volts
I would feel—would course through me.
That I would be so alive
To its cultural, technology and literary mores—
I would love the place as my own backyard.

That I would go climbing Mt Shasta and Mt Whitney,
Revel in Yosemite's storied rock-climbing history.
That I would ride my mountain bike,
Through the trails of North, South, and East Bays,
And I would learn, it's in Santa Cruz hills
Modern mountain biking took leaps.

That I would go skiing down the hills of Boreal and Mammoth
Mountains
I would go scuba diving down the Monterey coast.
I would imagine my tech-fueled life in the Silicon Valley
To be a singular, one grand experiment at work.

I take to these adventures
I write about places, life experiences and make poems
I would breathe this California air
And think about Beat, Bohemians and Geeks.

I would walk the streets
And feel the freedom, creativity and entrepreneurial vibes
I would feel that energy to explore and create something
Seek to create mass out of pure energy.
That each moment holds immensity
Of lurking possibilities, an acorn holding an oak tree in its
womb.
I see a commingling of ideas and cultures
This rich California soil yielded gold in the past
Birthed a poetry renaissance,
Shaped a liberal worldview and technological revolution—
I can be anything in this grandest place on Earth:
I can be an explorer, a technologist or a poet
That this place will shape my days to come,
Unbeknownst to me, I moved to California.

Coming Back to Big Sur

A summer dream, to run down
Narrow, winding, coastal Highway 1.
Don't hurry to make love, rather observe
Rising waves carried from ocean deep,
Caress the rugged shore of Big Sur passionately, in rhythmic
precision.

Same exact spot where we last made love,
Looking at the tired, roiling sea break upon its thirsty shore.
I tasted your lips within seventeen-mile drive,
I remember the taste of salt and sand,
I remember the humid and craggy Pebble beach.

I reach Bixby Canyon Bridge, the wild beauty,
California Dreaming ringing in my ear
And I think of Kerouac and Miller, loci of inspiration,
And Big Sur crystallizes for me in sharp relief,
Santa Lucia Mountains rise precipitously from the Pacific.

This time I am in no hurry to return home.
I come to see the inlands' redwoods, conifers, sycamores
I watch the mighty condors in the sky, gulls on the boulders
I have come to drink the intoxicating air
Pining for my daydream to manifest in the enchanting Big Sur.

A Santa Barbara Sunset

The sky is awash in golden rays, orange hues
Cast their net wide on the coastal Pacific waters.
The dazzling cliffs on the beach
Take a stance on the breaking waves.
A surfer is quick to paddle out of the rip currents, Campus
Point
Comes alive to the gradual, collective beats of its residents.

An evening cruise ship sets its sails in distant water, Santa
Barbara harbor
Comes home tonight
To its local wines and grand carousals.
Swaying palm trees sing of the sea and ancient mariners.
The evening is lit aglow against Santa Ynez Mountain
Sky—mountain and ocean one, giant, tangerine fireball.

Alone in San Francisco

Sauntering down the Embarcadero
Along the edges of pier 39,
A foggy morning clings to The City,
Rumbling itself awake from slumber
I trudge along the wooden pier,
Waves lap at the jetty,
Winds howl, a pelican nonchalantly
Flaps its wings and flies
Past my view ahead.

It's not so lonely, after all.
Nature resplendent in its spread today,
Winds, waves, ocean
Seem to have no bearing
To the seasons of my mind.
Nature is constant,
My mind shifts with each seed of thought.

I am not so lonely, after all
I open my arms
To welcome the oncoming wind,
Feel it directly on my face.
I let it caress my skin,
I feel it ruffle my hair,
And I close my eyes to
Witness the love of my friend.

I jump into the oncoming waves,
The Pacific blues
Cold as the thaw in my heart,
An instant commingling
Of two long lost lovers
For whom distance has not dimmed
Lights of their hearts.

Distant memory
Has a way of its own
To ebb and flow with the tide.
A dream
Can rise aflutter with the waves
Or sink to the bottom
With the changing tides
And time.

The ocean water—
I feared it may drown me.
Instead, it taught me how to swim
Along with the tide.

In the High Sierra

Dazzling mountain peaks, snow and rocks
Pierce through lenticular clouds,
Scattering the sunrays resplendently.
The grandeur of wilderness lights up my path.
My spirit soars at Mt Whitney,
Contemplating the vastness of its expanse.
The bastion of my heart lies breached at its glory.

Giant Sequoias rise
From the ground like a grand tower—
Snowmelts, alpine soil, and hundreds of years of time—all
caught in its labyrinth.
High above, the canopy of branches filters sunlight
Lighting up the forest like cathedral-stained-glass.

Lakes and waterfalls leap and roar,
Kissing meadows carved among mountains,
The natural spectacle of Yosemite and Kings Canyon,
Of Mirror lake and Roaring River Falls
Clambering down heart-shaped, deep valleys.

In this delight of an adventurer's arena
I have hiked and biked, rock climbed and bouldered,
Ridden on a horse through the Emigrant Wilderness.
My thirst for exhilarating quest,
Not fully sated, yet
I think of adventurous lives of John Muir and Mark Twain,
I think of the quaint towns of Bodie, Bishop and Twain Harte
And I think of the bygone era of the California Gold Rush—
Each treading a path through Time's changing seasons,
Passing eternally in this standstill citadel of the High Sierra.

Joshua Tree of Mojave

Arid, Mojave desert landscape,
Spartan, feisty under relentless Sun,
Austere rock outcrops, shrubs—
Wildflowers under a clear blue sky
Bloom vividly beneath a thousand stars
Under the cover of cold, dark night.
A solid trunk of a tree, a poetry
Unfurls its branches in a twisted scape,
Gazing straight upon the starry night,
In deep contemplation of its sparse existence.
Eking out a living of its own—
Resilient, the root seeks water through fault-lines of desert
Standing alone in sublime beauty of harsh climes,
Radiates joy to the lone hiker.
In the beauty of a silhouette, it emerges—
The Joshua tree of Mojave.

Mt Shasta Sunrise – A Mountaineering Quest

Frozen aeons rest easy on
The majestic snow-capped peak of Mt Shasta.
Time has chiseled the mountain in serenity.
I tread upon the couloir of time-slope, crampons on—
I wonder what fossils lurk in crevasses.
Night's shadow, air-chill, strong gusts—
My fear is cast upon these obstacles. My life story
Stands in a head-to-head battle with this mountain, a climax.

I lie down in my tent, cold night crawls upon Red Banks
In weariness, all thoughts float away like wind-blown mist,
I have tried and failed a thousand times by crack of dawn.
Unfazed, I open my eyes, ready to meet my mountain. My
adventurous spirit
Carves a roadmap to eternity on the snow-capped peak of Mt
Shasta.

Kayaking the Sea Caves in Channel Island

The ocean covers sky's vast space.
Dark grey clouds cast a reflection on the ominous water below
I paddle my Kayak amid rollicking waves,
Their undulating, rhythmic motion soothes my senses.
I am one with the ocean, all its waters,
All my thoughts drowned in its deep immensity.

I will paddle a little further, I tell myself.
The ethereal echo of my paddles slice the cold water,
Ricochet off stoic sea cliffs.
When I have nothing more to say, the downpour
Commences in full force. The water becomes one
From clouds to ocean—I marvel at the cycle of life.

Kayak, effortlessly glides in adventure's steady hands,
Desires to romp in the sea,
Stands bobbing at the narrow mouth of sea caverns
Off Scorpion Cove, Santa Cruz Island.

The dark cave faintly illuminates with rock-filtered light,
The gushing waves lash at rocks, the cave howls at me.
I try to steady my kayak, caught in the riff of the rapid currents.
A dash of fear leaps from the corners of the cave—
The ocean is vast in proportion to the dimensions of my skills.
I paddle out of the cave, navigating jutting cliffs and roaring
waves.
The cloud parts, the sky is lit with Sun again.
I pull near the shore, water flows in its elements.
Sky and ocean mingle in bright cobalt blue.

California Vibes

Everyone talks about chatGPT and OpenAI these days—
Silicon Valley of the nerds and techies crave
Musk, weed and crypto in no particular order.
That young lad sitting there quietly in Starbucks corner,
Will spin a software startup all from the screen of his laptop.
Investors
Of A16z, Sequoia fame, will hone their attention looking for the
next Google, Meta
Fishing for the gold, in his 'hockey-stick' growth-frenzied pitch.

In LA, every writer carries a movie script in his pocket
And every actor is looking for a famed Hollywood producer.
A dream is born every minute and fights its chances in the
streets,
Love blooms, music flows, Sebastian and Mia waltz through a la
La La Land.

Further south, in San Diego, the Sun rests easy on Pacific
coastal waters,
A surfer pulls his surf board from his van in La Jolla Shores.
Nearby, La Jolla Cove is teeming with divers, snorkelers,
swimmers.
The zeal of an adventurer's heart can wander untamed unto
Death Valley, in the neigh.

Disruptive technology, creativity, the call of the adventure,
The three cities of California vibe with each other equally well.
I have seen the techie flamboyance of San Francisco in the
creative soul of LA,
I found the same outdoorsy thirst of San Diego in the
quenchable waters of SF.

Arrival—In "The City"

They say a city is defined
By its skyline.
I don't believe it. The City
Is a throbbing heart of
People and their culture.
However, I cannot escape
Noticing the distinct shape of
The Transamerica pyramid
Piercing through San Francisco's skyline.

Crawling in traffic, on the
Golden Gate Bridge, I head back
To The City from Marin,
I marvel at the rust-red
Trusses of massive bridge towers,
Peering down through clouds.
The City descends upon my arrival
Surreptitiously
Like rip currents,
Of Pacific, that breaks near the shore.

Soon I may be swallowed whole,
By the distinct charm
Of Chinatown, Fillmore or the Haight-Ashbury.
Or I may emerge
From the bowels of a big wave,
Like an experienced surfer
Enjoying the surf-ride of his life.
The charm of The City
Is marked by numerous
Waves, ebbing and flowing
With the tides of the Pacific.

A Place of My Own

I have rummaged through my belongings,
Searching for the anchor
To my coarsened soul.
Looking down at my baggage,
Seeking in the places I have been to,
In the recesses of my heart and in the nooks of my memories
I have looked all around, but in vain.

I have looked over the mountains,
I have looked in the depths of the oceans,
Ridden through the valleys and the pines,
In search of that place, that I may call my own.
I took a Paraglide by the Pacific,
I hiked alone in the wilderness,
Skied down the snowy slopes,
Quietly, looking for a place of my own.
I am not an explorer, still my heart aches
For the far-away places, reticent
Nestled rightly in the wilderness.

A Poet Animated in San Francisco

We've left our home,
Come this far out, searching.
We are forever lost,
What holds any charm in The City?

When this October dawn breaks over the Embarcadero
Will you jog down its side-walks?
Fully awake, you couldn't sleep
Keeping company with your old memories.

Thick fog, cover of cloud, thoughts and hopes
Envelope The City like a shroud on the body,
The decay of yesterday has given in to the high-rises of
tomorrow,
Will you leave for home today or find a way to live another day
in The City?

O San Francisco, you gave voice to Beats,
You made art in the Mission.
Your Bohemian vibe lives on
In the poet who dreams of The City
And countryside, both in equal measure.

Litquake* —October 2022

Out of the voices of Beat poetry,
    Out of the art deco at Mission Street,
Out of the swirls of the Pacific,
    Out of the foggy cover of the Golden Gate Bridge,
The vibe of The City grows upon me, day by day.

The City, a poem
Waiting for the poet to sing its lore
The City, a muse
Waiting for the Orchestra conductor to direct its choir.
Living, breathing, pulsating with character
Story be told, history be unveiled
San Francisco lives in you, when you breathe in its air.

At Southern Exposure, a crowd gathers, poets assemble,
Images hang on the walls, voices hang in the air.
Thoughts collide, ideas float,
Pages turn, poems emerge.
Out of this emotionally-charged air
A notion is conceived
Of a seashell—life comes around in a spiral.
Not a circle per-se,
Not quite returning to the same place
But not quite too far from where it all started.
City life is a seashell.
You can't develop escape velocity to go far from its gravity.
At San Francisco Litquake,
Poets return to the seashell of new ideas,
Year after another year.

Footnote: Litquake is San Francisco's annual literary festival

At Pillar Point Harbor, Half Moon Bay

The gray cloud looms over Pillar Point
Like a threatening lion
Ready to charge upon
An unsuspecting prey.
Pacific swells in blues and grays
Breaking its charm upon the shore.
A sail boat is ready to dock
Pulling itself gingerly into the harbor,
Ready to throw its buoy,
I try to recollect
How a Larkis knot is made.

An ocean has myriad moods—
It's said that
Ships crash the most
Near a harbor.
Perhaps the sight of shore
Catches a sailor in a hurry,
Pushing forth to return to land's comfort.
Ironic—sailors who navigate turbulent waters in Deep Ocean
Get blind-sided by shallow waters.
At Pillar Point today, I seek equanimity in all my actions.

Horse Riding in Half Moon Bay

Blackjack is a fast ride,
I hear the horse trainer called from behind me.
My horse is trotting delicately on the trail.
Holding the rein, I sit astride.

I must be a light rider—
Blackjack canters ahead.
Wind sweeps over my face,
Clearing my mind of day's residuals.

The trail merges in hazy woods ahead
Pacific waters shine on the blue sky,
The shadow of my heart thaws away
I feel effortless.

I look ahead in anticipation,
A sliver of mist appears on distant horizon.
Unbridled by yesterday's weight,
I tuck my feet straight into the stirrup.

Blackjack gallops ahead,
Carrying my weight into the dusk,
My head unburdened,
In a weightless bliss,
Sauntering in the woods,
Despite raging headwinds.

At Mt Whitney

The majestic mountain stands tall
Piercing the azure sky
With its jagged peaks.

Snow on the slopes
Casts an erringly white hue
As if white velvet would quietly
Meld into blue sky.

The wind shivers its way
Beneath my skin.
A luminous silence hangs
like a necklace around Whitney.

Just above the camp at Trail Crest
Tree line appears, jagged marker.
In the high altitude of mountains,
The daily routines of my normal world
Dissolve in mist.

In my camp at night
I lie in the sleeping bag—
Dark sky lit with stars...
Nature unfolds in the wilderness, unhindered.

Of Beats, Bohemians and Bukowski *

When Jack Kerouac wrote
On the Road, he was a
Bohemian traveler seeking
Respite from weariness
In the sinuous Pacific stretch
From Big Sur to the North Beach.
Poetry emerged from living ordinary lives.
Beat was born in San Francisco.

That free-spirit vibe,
That bon-homie,
That c'est la vie—
It's time to feel the energy again
Waltzing through North Beach bohemia
Down to the singular Burning man.

'Find something you love
And let it kill you', wrote
Charles Bukowski.
He was not speaking of
Poetry alone.
He posed a question directly to us,
Asking resolutely—
Have you found your slow poison, yet?
Have you tasted the slow burn of your raging passion?
Have you gone far out, chasing your aspiration?

Footnote: The Beat Generation was a literary subculture movement started by a group of authors whose work explored and influenced American culture and politics in the post-World War II era, in 1950s and 60s with San Francisco as the major hub. Jack Kerouac was a prominent in shaping the Beat Generation.

Jet Skiing in Lake Tahoe

I take my jet ski from the marina
At Emerald Bay
Gingerly crossing the lines of boats and skis
Floating, lolling up and down with the gentle crashing waves.
The clear, turquoise water of Lake Tahoe
Set amid the rolling hills,
The air feels lighter, I am told
It's 6000 ft above sea level. Serenity prevails.

I enter deep water in the lake's middle,
My right hand raring
To feel power of the Jet Ski engine.
Yamaha Waverunner is no mean machine,
Designed akin to a motorcycle, engineered to crush the waves.

My heart does a dance
As I pull in the throttle:
Boom!
I go riding the waves, leaving a white streak of water behind.
I am riding the Jet Ski
In the deep, dark blue waters of Lake Tahoe,
Leaving my orderly world behind
To an adventurous life lived on the waters—
Guess this summer shouldn't end soon.

Berkeley Half-Marathon

Your spirit is meant to soar
And the mind, an apogee of Zen.
Your body is meant to race swift,
Let those legs take every step
Firm, determined and relentless.
Let those knees take the blows
Of the hard pavement or the trail.

You may get tired—
Rest you may, but stop you may not.
Run until you breathe heavily,
Run until your heart beats fast,
Run until you feel shaken—
Still run, until you complete the race.

Let your mind guide your soul
Let your body get into the zone.
Hit the dust with both your feet,
Calm, but raging inside until the end.

Let your soul soak in adrenaline
Let your mind nurture the spirit
Let your body feel euphoria
Sponging on the 'runner's high,'
Further determined to race again.

High on Poetry & Caffeine

Not perchance
That Beats emerged in San Francisco,
When Jack Kerouac traversed the breadth of America
He found his respite in the arms of The City.

High on caffeine
40 miles south
In the heart of 'Silicon Valley' of today,
I troll by writing poems, among the nerds, the founders
And people who code.
I am an antithesis
Of the coder types.
I belong here by the day
When I go to my job,
Yet I don't.
The technical problem of 'cloud migration'
Holds my attention enough
To look for a solution.
Within the freedom of words
And story of art and artists
That I relish being alive
To the music of Beat verses and Bukowski,
Floating in the valley of San Francisco Bay—
Even to these days, for those who will listen.

Sailing in Oakland Estuary

The gentle breeze lifts my spirits
Feels as light as the sails of the twenty-three foot boat
Sailing the waves on blue Pacific
Embarking from the Oakland estuary.

The white clouds part to reveal azure sky
As turquoise as ocean water, melding over the horizon.
The shrill horn of a massive cargo ship fills the air,
I grab my tiller tightly,
Ready to tack away in its wake.

The currents lap at the hull,
The wind pushes against its majestic sails.
Caught between these two forces,
We dance in the ocean, balancing our world at almost a 20
degree tilt.

Soon the estuary opens in the deep, open waters of the Pacific,
The Bay Bridge beckoning us rapidly,
The gusts of wind gathering strength.
Tacking and jibing under the bridge waters,
We set sail on our course—
Alive to the adventures that lie ahead.

Adventures in Reading - Santa Clara City Library

I walk down the aisles, the stacks,
Picking a copy of *The Moth And The Mountain*
And I travel a few hours with Maurice Wilson
On a mountaineering journey to India, Tibet, Everest.

Atlantic took me on a heroic sailing trip across the ocean,
The Boys In The Boat told of a glorious quest for the Rowing
Olympic gold.
Flipping pages, I journey, I become
A traveler, An explorer,
Ready to set sail across oceans,
Or dive into the waters to uncover the world of the deep.
I embark on my own expeditions,
Courage and adventure set my tempo.

My soul set free, my imagination on fire.
Reading in Santa Clara city library
I have grown wings
To soar, glide, fly—higher.

Scuba Diving in Monterey

The morning wind blows across my face,
I raise my gaze to the horizon,
My eyes drift across the bay,
Ocean and sky meld, revealing a wider panorama.

I feel much lighter
Scuba gear on my back notwithstanding.
Waves and the ocean
Cure the blues in my mind.

I put on the dive mask,
Adjust the buoyancy control device,
And dive beneath incessant waves,
Drawing the breath of my Nitrox.

My eyes feast on underwater scenery:
Rich and vibrant colors abound in the kelp, anemones, corals.
Sunlight filters through the water
Like a kaleidoscope. I bask in Sun's warmth
And water's cold.

Gliding weightless,
I feel the calmness of water surrounding my sentience.
My eyes open up to a new world—
I have never seen Zen before, in its essence.

The Mist

Bone-chilling cold and
The Sun up in San Francisco—
Thick mist of morning
I'm driving on I-80 Highway,
Leaving yesterday behind
Staring at bright golden towers
Rising from waters in the mouth of the bay,
Set against the Marin headlands.
My swirling thoughts bound
By the panorama unfolding,
Too stunned to draw any conclusion.
Silence lies scattered, I am going nowhere.
Yesterday done, I tell myself.

Sun's golden rays disperse
Thick mist hovering over the towers.
My desires shining on the horizon
In the breaking dawn, glistening,
Marin hills in solitude,
Breaking waves of the Pacific
Arrested by foothills, stony
Stoic, calm no match for the ocean.
A ray of hope for tomorrow,
Pries open my wounded heart.
I drive calmly
Over the bridge, to the Marin.
I reach where I intend to arrive.

Of Metallica, Green Day, Jefferson Airplane

That Metallica concert in July 2015
Hit such high notes at AT&T Park *
Those swells, crowd roars
That music buzzing in my chest,
Nothing else mattered.
Jefferson Airplane
Sang psychedelic *White Rabbit*
And I got lost in the labyrinth of music and San Francisco
sound
I hadn't taken red or blue pills.
Toughening up, I found myself
Looking for Alice in the Matrix.
When Green Day tripp'd on
Boulevard of Broken Dreams, and chose to walk alone
The Bay shook and people across the world noted
It was no longer a lonely road!

Footnote: AT&T Park is now called Oracle Park

Cannery Row and Monterey

With no particular objective,
It feels pleasant to stroll along the blocks of Cannery Row,
Admiring the bustling shops, row of restaurants and cool cafes,
Air abuzz, aroma floats of ocean, fish and chocolates.

A place keeps its own history: birth, renewal, and maturity
I am not oblivious to John Steinbeck's eponymous novel,
His literary tale of human conditions and camaraderie still
vibrant
In the streets, to every discerning eye, who cares to look far and
beyond.

Last time I went to Monterey Bay
I was taken with scuba diving,
The water is twice as deep as the Grand Canyon.
And I learned of Monterey Canyon, hiding deep beneath the
coastal waters.
I wonder what other secrets lie hidden in Monterey.
What other beauties, not yet seen and what other stories not yet
told.

Jack London State Historic Park, Sonoma

The rolling hills of Sonoma gently give way to
Passing mists in the wee hours of morning
The mountain bike trail ebbs and flows in the verdant greenery
around
The stone façade of 'Wolf House' standing in stoic silence,
I wonder, had Jack London inhabited his *Beauty Ranch*
What other adventurous tales he would have told the world?
What more anecdotes of his sailing days would he have inked?
I wonder if the air in Sonoma still bears his literary mark.
I listen closely, lending my ear to the passing breeze
For an echo of *The Call of the Wild.*

On the Road – influenced by Jack Kerouac

I didn't mean to leave home
Ever, I was bound by my desires to wander
I had to go somewhere.
Somewhere where the rolling hills spoke
To the clouds and the valley below
Echoed my name
As sun-kissed wind swept it clean.

I got into my car and drove west—
West, where California grandeur lay
Stretched across the Pacific waters.
And the city of San Francisco rose misty-eyed
Over the Golden Gate every morning.

I dreamt of jazz clubs and steamy sex,
Road trips. Scribbling through the heat of the night
I think of Dean Moriarty—
How old and weary he would have been
Of the vicissitudes of life, or
Would he be happy, contented,
Having lived through his carefree youth?
Not to be contented with
Mere wandering of thoughts,
I am on the road again,
Going to meet my lost pal, Sal
Sal Paradise.

Sunny California

It rained incessantly today,
A grey cloud just drifted across my window-
I sit at my desk, jotting notes,
Rain pitter-patters on my window panes,
The cyclical, repetitive rhythm....
It's already January 1, 2023,
California winters can be rainy,
The draught-struck land can finally find some respite.
Collecting my scattered thoughts,
I feel calm, I sing to myself.
Rain has unclogged the drainage,
And washed my window panes, afresh
When the clouds drift away tomorrow,
The Sun shall set my freshly-bathed room aglow.
I will look out my window and say—
It's always sunny in California!

The Lighthouse at the End of the Road
– Point Reyes

The solitary lighthouse
On the craggy shoreline of Point Reyes
Stands tall, a sentry in vigil
Guarding ships to safe passage,
Imbued with altruistic dedication.
I wonder what it takes to keep calm in a hurricane.
Howling wild wolves, the waves,
My mind blanks out, the turmoil.

The other day,
I withered away, tired and lost
Navigating through the dense City of fog
I lost the way,
Despite my career compass
My North Star,
Invisible to me,
I was looking for my lighthouse
To shine a beacon, in vain.

Point Reyes, flash your light
To the lost souls of humanity
Washed ashore
Treading through their daily drudgery,
Despite their ships anchored on the coast—
Many a hope lost.

The Places We Inhabit - A Pantoum

There is something in the air of California,
I have spent my thirties belonging here.
My parents have grown old in another land,
What was it about California that made me stay?

I have spent my thirties living here,
Nurturing my sense of adventure in Tahoe, Monterey and
environs,
What was it about California that made me stay?
I thought I had found my answer when I chose to build a home.

I have nurtured my sense of adventure in Tahoe, Monterey and
environs,
Yet my body is full of longing for a distant land.
I thought I had found my answer when I chose to build a home,
To my disbelief, the passing years added up too soon, fifteen to
be exact.

My body is full of longing for the distant land,
Who thought that my parents would grow old?
The passing years added up too soon, fifteen to be exact.
I inhabited two worlds together, one in the body and the other
in the mind.

Who thought that my parents would grow old?
I remember what my mother told me before I left.
All these years, I inhabited two worlds together, one in the body
and the other in the mind.
The body accreted layers of memory from California, the mind
remained fossilized since fifteen years from the distant land.

I remember what my mother told me before I left,
There is something in the air of California.
The body accreted layers of memory from California, the mind
remained fossilized since fifteen years from the distant land,
My parents have grown old in another land.

Skiing at Boreal, Tahoe

The day is enveloped in snowfall's daze
Grey-covered sky and snow-white slopes,
Winds blow cold and still I must go.
I fasten the wings on my skis
With a thumping heart, I leap off the chair lift.
The powder moves beneath my feet,
I tighten my gloves, put goggles on,
The rush of freedom courses through my veins
Carving the slope with my skis, I set myself downhill.
Adrenaline and exhilaration overtake me.

Down the slope, I look back to the mountain—
Nature's paint-brush strokes a grand canvas,
And the ski trail of my last run on the freshies—
Artist and adventurer passions commingle in downhill skiing.

Sausalito Summer on a Motorcycle

The Golden Gate Bridge, down south in Frisco,
Congested this morning, whittles down
Traffic steadily pouring in
Onto the alleys of sunny Sausalito.

My wandering desires with me, long before
I come to Sausalito through Frisco and
This gatekeeper, the bridge simply relents to me.

I ride my motorcycle over the bridge
And through the rainbow tunnel,
Eyes on the road and ears on the sweeping
Vistas and dazzling Blue Ocean.
The twists and turns of the winding Sausalito streets,
Impart an additional exhilaration to my ride.
I steer my motorcycle up the hill and down to Ferry Landing.
Cruising along the breezy, Bridgeway Promenade,
I let my eyes behold the ecstasy of countless sailboats,
Carousing in the ocean in absolute abandon,
White masts gleaming against the contours of curvy sky.

Enchanted by the cool waterfront,
I devour the Bohemian air of Sausalito.
My vagabond heart
Beating a path
Through Sausalito summer,
Finds its abode, riding a motorcycle to nirvana.

When Thrill Overcomes Fear

Dancing on the edge of anxiety,
I pull my bike through
The curve on the mountain pass.
Riding high on adrenaline, I push through
Without using the brake
Steering my 'Thunder' across the crest.

Coming onto a straight road,
I roll my throttle,
Grab my clutch and shift to sixth—
I let speed overtake
The fear in my bones.

Distance passes quickly in a whirr, roar of engine
Soothes my nerves—
It's calm inside my helmet, the wind-howl outside.
Dancing on the edge of fear,
I push past one hundred miles an hour.
The thrill of the roaring 'Thunder'
Pulsating between my thighs
Has crossed its way
Beyond, my mountain of fear.

I relax by riding, notwithstanding
The passing fear, juxtaposed
Continuously against my nerve.

Devil's Backbone, Mt Baldy

Climb the mountain, a self-respecting man
Should carry one's own baggage
Experience what it's like
To shoulder the weight of responsibilities

Negotiate the uneven terrain of foothills deftly,
Begin to move up quickly, higher elevation
Open up new vistas, enchanting for my weary eyes.
Beyond the ski hut, ground swells upward
A more dramatic gradient, climb uphill is punishing.

Carry on, stoic to one's own suffering
Trail mark reveals, approaching Devil's backbone
A narrow ridge, sheer vertical exposures on both sides of cliff
Gathering clouds pick up speed, ominous and dark sky.

Wind pierces my exposed face, I pluck my courage
Scrambling through the devil's backbone, unfettered.
Nausea of high altitude, fear of sheer vertical drop
Sit pretty on my shoulder, the weight of my baggage lightened.
Touched by height of the mountain, higher elevation
Unveil the lightness of my being. A serene, blissful morning

Time Is a False Measure

Time is a false measure
Everyone has their own journey.
Does it really matter,
Who arrives first, or who reaches last?

There is no destination,
Just a medley of pursuit and idleness
Between milestones,
Making the travel poignant,
Ascribing some meaning
To each heart's desire.

I seek not to reach
Anywhere.
But I seek to be on a journey
Continually,
Without baggage of any regret or hope
Without any guilt of time elapsed
Subsumed in the experience of the voyage.
When will I reach?
I seek not to know,
For time is a false measure.
There is no destination,
There is no arrival.

Napa Valley

...and the wine is bottled poetry...
—Robert Louis Stevenson

The gently rolling hills,
Verdant greenery of vineyards,
Blossoming wilderness,
A longing heart-beat
All deeply ensconced under an
Ochre-colored, cirrus sky.
Napa, Calistoga,
St. Helena, Yountville,
With rich bounty,
Basking in distinct essence.

Napa Valley,
A lavish Paradise,
Distilled and diligently conserved
In every bottle of Wine.
Napa Valley Vintners
Thus, write a poem to
Each connoisseur, for every
Wine bottle that's uncorked.

LA Musings and Celluloid Dreams

A slice of daydream,
Unforgettable storyline
Born under swaying palms
Of an art-deco Santa Monica,
The writer spins his narrative in LA.
Down the Sunset Boulevard
He will take a stroll in creative amazement
And spend another idle day—
Hollywood Walk of Fame
Venting cinematic desires,
Rapt in a nascent ambition,
He gawks at Beverly Hills or Bel Air,
Think of Chandler* and Bukowski**.

He may change his storyline,
Time and again, to fit his muse
Of the moment. With a canvas
Of celluloid dreams,
Sepia-tinted—
Once upon a time in Hollywood—
Banking upon his past and future.
Success and fame.

In his frenzy,
The writer roams the hills and boulevards,
Freeways crisscrossing the sprawling
City of Dreams, Los Angeles.
Wresting with longings, heart-aches and celluloid dreams.

*Footnote: * Raymond Chandler , ** Charles Bukowski*

On California

I see California, through the eyes of gold-rush prospectors,
And I see the courage to leave the comfort of home behind
To venture out into an unknown terrain for a better future.

I see California, through the eyes of Beat poets,
And I see the determination to reject mainstream materialism,
To embark on a quest to pursue arts, Zen and spiritual
philosophy.

I see California, through the eyes of Hollywood dream-
merchants,
And I see remarkable creativity and ingenuity of story-telling,
Entertaining, inspiring and influencing millions across the
world.

I see California, through the eyes of Silicon Valley technology
czars,
And I see exceptional innovations, new-age startups, and
businesses
Shaping the collective future of human-kind for the days to
come.

I see California, through the eyes of progressive citizens,
And I see strong conviction in the values of diversity, equality,
and inclusivity,
Holding a beacon for tolerance, free-thinking, and open-
mindedness.

I see California through my own eyes,
And I see mountains and ocean, iconic Yosemite and Big Sur
Calling the adventurer, dreamer, and poet in each of us,
To explore, push forth through obstacles, and write our own
story.

Afterword

The Poem *Alone in San Francisco* was selected to be first published in San Francisco Writers Conference 2022 Writing Contest Anthology called *Everything Intensely*

Epilogue

"When you feel that you are done
Go outdoors, explore in the sun
Lift your eyes unto those distant hills
A challenge calls, an adventure awaits"

- Lalit Kumar,
from 'Years Spent: Exploring Poetry in Adventure,
Life and Love'

www.ingramcontent.com/pod-product-compliance
Lightning Source LLC
Chambersburg PA
CBHW051002140626
46546CB00017B/2657